HOW TO THINK MUSIC

By

HARRIET AYER SEYMOUR

FOURTH EDITION
REVISED AND AUGMENTED

"The culture we recommend is, above all, an inward operation."
—MATTHEW ARNOLD

G. SCHIRMER, INC., NEW YORK

Copyright, 1910, by THE H. W. GRAY CO.

First published in
THE NEW MUSIC REVIEW

Copyright, 1915, by
G. SCHIRMER, INC.
25716

Printed in the U. S. A.

To Dr. Frank Damrosch

whose efforts for the advancement of music in America have been untiring

PREFACE.

In music, as in other things, we have allowed ourselves to do a great deal of thoughtless, and therefore useless work. The object of this book is to arouse those who have only played music to think music before playing it. The thought must always be prior to the fact. The inward process of listening and hearing is not adequately expressed by the word think, but it seems to be the best term descriptive of the process that the English language affords.

I do not presume for a moment to address myself to the trained musician to whom this side of the question has become second nature, but rather to the lover of music who has played the piano or organ or any other musical instrument, and who has never really heard inwardly (or thought) the music he has played. Since so many persons of the latter class have enriched their lives already after the manner herein advocated, the temptation to write this book has proved irresistible.

I am under obligations to Professor William P. Trent, of Columbia College, whose helpful suggestions and criticisms have been of the utmost value to me. I wish also to thank my pupils, whose interest and enthusiasm have been unfailing.

H. A. S.

NEW YORK, August, 1910.

CONTENTS

Chapter I.	Introductory	7
Chapter II.	Melody	11
Chapter III.	Rhythm	29
Chapter IV.	Chords	38
Addenda		53
Teaching Material		55

How To Think Music.

CHAPTER I.

INTRODUCTORY.

THIS little book, the outgrowth of my own experience in teaching music, is a plea for two things: First, that we shall strive to enable our students to work from principles; and, secondly, that we shall present the study of music so simply that the student will be definitely conscious of what he learns.

It is not what the teacher intends to convey that takes root in the mind of the pupil, but what the pupil understands. In my judgment there is really no such thing as taking piano lessons. The piano is simply the instrument we choose for the expression of musical ideas. Music itself is in the mind, and therefore the teaching of it should be distinctly a mental training. How many thousand students of music have given up in despair because they had never been taught to think music!

My first realization of this came to me in the following way: A friend and I had undertaken the teaching of kitchen gardening in a settlement school class. Neither of us had had any experience, and we found the children very unteachable. While we were racking our

Illustration of Bad Methods

brains for some means of quieting them, I thought of music. My friend was a brilliant pianist.

"You play some familiar song and I'll make them sing," I said.

"I have no notes," she answered.

"But play anything—play 'My Country, 'Tis of Thee.'"

"I have no notes," she still retorted. Whereupon I sat down at the piano and soon had the children quiet and contented.

On the way home I asked my friend to explain her conduct, and she confessed that she was absolutely lost at the keyboard unless she had notes or knew the music from having "memorized" it. The playing and harmonizing of a simple melody was an impossibility to her and yet she was called "a very fine musician."

We should be taught to think music, and there necessarily must be a definite principle to work from. For instance, instead of making the pupil learn in a year, perhaps, to play six "pieces," it would be far better to establish in his mind certain definite facts from which he can work always, such as:

Working Principles

First—Hearing the tones inwardly before producing them.

Second—Finding the tones on the keyboard in all keys.

Third—Realizing the scale relationship and

intervals so that all keys are equally easy for him.

Fourth—Learning the principle that underlies rhythm.

Fifth—Singing and writing simple original melodies which he has heard inwardly first, and last of all harmonizing these melodies.

In two or three years it ought to be and is possible for him to play and harmonize any simple melody, in any key; to be conscious of exactly what is taking place, both in his mind and on the keyboard, and to play good simple music, understanding its fundamental harmony and feeling its rhythm. This is not a new idea, for many teachers are applying it already. The demand for more vital teaching is growing among parents; the children themselves prefer it.

Grown-up people who have "studied music" and then given it up in despair because they never seemed to acquire any working basis for independent study, are taking it up again in this way, so novel to them.

Some Good Results

Because of the effects of the new teaching it is becoming less common for a girl to give up music when she marries. She certainly needs then all that is beautiful and ennobling, needs it as much, if not more, than ever before. This "new education" in music means music in the home. We do not, as a people, want so much the brilliant performer as we want mothers who can and will play for the children to dance and sing; who, if the notes are not at hand, understand the principles so well that they can play without notes, and who can, if necessary, transpose a little song into the key that suits the childish voices.

We need more music in the world, because we need more culture, more beauty, more sweetness, and music makes for all of these.

It may be a fanciful idea, but I believe that music is an absolute necessity to an harmonious development. True culture must include music, and since "men of culture are the true apostles of equality," music is a force or power for social good, and should be taught with the utmost clearness and simplicity. Experience has shown me that children, and older persons as well, who have been taught in this way, love music more and more. The time is always too short, and the hours at the piano do not by any means constitute the whole of music to the student. It is an ever present element in his life and in the lives of those about him. To every one should be given the chance to cultivate this inherent sense for beauty of sound, in such a way as to make it a permanent help towards a more harmonious and joyous life.

CHAPTER II.

MELODY.

 piano lesson must include thought as well as action. Heretofore too much attention has been paid to more or less mechanical movements of the hands and arms, and too little to the heart of the subject. When their attention is called to it, many students are astonished to find how little music they really hear, mentally.

Thought and Action

The study of music, to be of any value, must consist, first of all, of an inward process. The ability to think music or to hear it inwardly is the root of the problem. In other words, the study of music must take place primarily in the mind. The first step should be to hear, mentally, a very simple melody, not to hear it played on the instrument, but to hear it inwardly—not "with the mind's eye," but with the mind's ear, so to speak, and then to reproduce outwardly what is heard, by singing it. If the pupil can learn to listen, the music is there waiting. For instance, start by singing such a simple combination of tones as:

and ask the pupil to give you one equally simple. Let him—

    1—inwardly hear it.
    2—sing it.
    3—find it on the keyboard.
    4—write it down.

This is fascinating to all students, although there is sometimes trouble in making a start. "It is the first step that costs the most." It is better to confine one's self to the simplest music for some time, and to be sure to hear the melody very distinctly before you sing and play and write it. Once a student has learned to hear music mentally the flood-gates of melody are open to him.

Words are sometimes used with these first melodies. Mr. Calvin B. Cady, to whose book, "Music Education," I refer all those who wish to take up this side of the question more fully, considers this very important. In my opinion it is an individual matter. We are studying tones, and the sound alone is enough if the pupil can thus become conscious of melody. Children usually prefer to use words. Sometimes a phrase, such as:

Use of Words

"Pitter, patter, goes the rain."

or a quotation from a familiar verse, as:

"The organ with the organ man
  Is singing in the rain."

proves helpful.

Every lesson for a long time should include this melody work until the pupil can think a

melody easily; sing it, write it and play it. It
is always a delight to discover
Thinking Melodies that one can unearth such a wealth of tunes in one's own mind. I have watched this process in all sorts of persons and been obliged sometimes to train so-called "monotones" into recognizing and producing the seven tones before getting to tunes. With patience it can be done. Work according to Froebel's principle that within the pupil is the consciousness of music, and that the teacher's work is to stimulate the awakening of that consciousness.

There are, of course, many ways—just as many ways as there are obstacles. For instance, one boy refuses to sing—let him whistle. Another refuses even
No Set Rule for Teaching to whistle—says he "can't"—let him start by picking out familiar tunes on the keyboard. Another "hates" this but loves the opera; let him find some melody or motif on the keyboard. The best way is first, listening; second, singing; third, writing; fourth, playing; but there is absolutely no set rule to be laid down because individuals are not sheep, and must be met on their own ground. Therefore, the order may be changed sometimes, provided the pupil has heard the melody first. This is imperative. It matters very little whether in a year a pupil has heard, sung and written one hundred melodies or five, if only he has become conscious

of melody in his own mind and can produce what he has heard.

A friend of mine sent me her little daughter. The child, artistic to her very finger tips, had been "learning to play the piano" for six years and hated music. I got her to show me her work. She had written out, absolutely mechanically, books of notes which had no meaning whatever to her and which were simply records of dull and unprofitable hours unwillingly given to music. Her playing was perfunctory because she disliked the cheap, modern things she played. Altogether, she was a good example of the results of a perfectly uninteresting, external and mechanical mode of teaching "music."

Two Different Ways

Finally, I asked her whether she had ever done anything in her music work that interested her. Smilingly she produced a sheet of paper brought from school on which was written:

"I wrote it myself," she said, "I loved to do it and I can sing it." This one little piece of really thoughtful work had stamped itself indelibly on her mind and made her happy. Teachers will find that all children are interested in thinking music and that the interest grows where otherwise it is apt to flag.

It is Emerson, I think, who says that the really great man is he who dwells on the affirmative, positive side of things, and so it is

Interest of Pupils

with the teacher. The teacher must meet the pupil on some congenial ground. For instance, if the pupil always has wanted to "pick things out" on the piano, the teacher should find out the music he is interested in and let him pick that out. If he has difficulty in playing it he will be willing soon to think and sing it first, because he desires to play it. Thus he will see the use of singing. "Desire is the soul of will." Actual work with every imaginable kind of child, from the "unmusical," "uninterested," "stubborn," "nervous" kind to the interested musical and willing one, has proven the truth of this statement.

When I first started to teach some apparently hopeless pupils were given me, but their interest, once aroused, has never wavered.

How to Arouse Interest

One boy whose mother brought him to me as a last resort—a pitched battle with his teacher having been the final episode of his stormy career as a would-be "performer" on the much-abused and long-suffering piano—now talks of composing an opera, and was quite insistent about having a lesson on Christmas day because that happened to be his regular time for a lesson, and he couldn't bear to miss it. The fact is that when true music thinking is aroused, it never can be forgotten or neglected.

Two or three years ago I was asked to take a desperate case, a little girl who came of a musical family, who had had lessons all her life, and who had fought regularly with her distracted teacher.

"I am told," said the mother, "that you will help Mary to love her music, but I must tell you that she is unwilling and disobedient, and if you can interest her I shall be surprised."

At first it was uphill work, but by studying the child's tastes I managed to stir up a spark of interest. All singing and note writing was unpleasant to her, so that she simply played some Schumann and Mozart, for the first six months. Gradually the love of music grew. Finally she asked me to teach her harmony, and even begged for extra hours, and this year she has laid a foundation that will never leave her, and on which she is building already. This foundation consisted first of all of thinking, singing and writing and playing melodies.

Through mental photography certain necessary facts may be impressed upon the mind. A clear mental image consciously made is invaluable in the study of music. Take the very simplest facts which we are obliged to know in order to read music easily: First of all the notes. Place the chart before the pupil. Let him look at it intently, then close his eyes and mentally see—middle C—in its position between the staves, and then—"twice lined C"—above and below.

Have him repeat this process until he can write out from memory what he has seen. Then take up the next point, i. e., the position of the notes on the two staves, and impress it mentally in the same way. (See ADDENDA, p. 53.)

Writing from Memory

Then the next—to teach the values of notes and rests. Have the child see the chart, first of all, with the physical eye, and afterward with the mind's eye. One might term it conscious mental photography.

Values of Notes and Rests

NOTES.

RESTS.

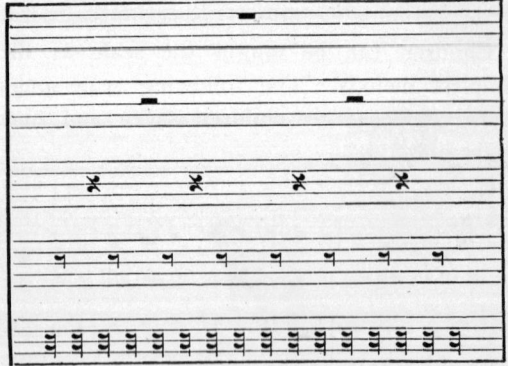

The next step is the transposing of melodies. As soon as you can think a melody, you should be able to transpose it. The tones of which melodies consist are, of course, made up of tones of the scale. Since the scale is the basis of all melodic thought, it must be studied thoroughly and with understanding.

The Scale

The diatonic scale exists in the consciousness. We come to feel that the scale is an established and logical relationship, just as two and two are four is an established and logical relationship—just as the multiplication table is an established and logical relationship. It is not necessary to explain why this is so, it is sufficient that it is so. In order to transpose melodies, we must be absolutely at home in singing, writing and playing the scale in all keys.

Children can be taught the scale as the simplest melody. The following scale-songs were composed by children seven and nine years old.

The fish are swimming all a-round Because they can't walk on the ground.

I have a bird who sings all day, He nev-er sings when I'm a-way.

The rain is rain-ing all a-round, Up-on the trees and on the ground.

Therefore let the children make scale songs, using their own words, or words given by the teacher, and let them sing these same songs in another key, *i. e.,* transpose them. Suppose, for instance, that a child is familiar with the C scale only, can hear, sing, write and play it. Let him play D, for instance, as the first note, and find the scale. He will play D, E, F natural, but quickly hear that F natural is not the tone he wants. Then he will find F sharp and know that it sounds as he wants to hear it; then follow G, A, C. C sounds out of harmony with the other notes, and he quickly puts his finger on C-sharp, then D, and he has discovered the scale of D for himself.

Finding the Scales

Let him discover all of the scales in this way. Let him write each scale that he discovers and indicate the half-steps. Thus he will see that the form is a half-tone at 3 and 4 and the same at 7 and 8. Proceeding in this way, it is plain that it is the sound that counts, and that the form is the outcome of the sound. Dwell on this point.

This discovery of the scale in different places teaches many things: the sound of it, the form of it, and that it does not matter at all whether there are two flats or six sharps in it—it is always the same scale of eight perfectly related tones, as easy to deal with in one key as another. Most pupils ask why you call a note sharp and not flat, or vice versa. For instance, take the key of G: why, when you have played G, A, B, C, D, E, must it be F-sharp? Why not G-flat? Simply because the scale consists of eight tones, and each tone must have its own name. We have had E, and G is the last tone, so we must have F something, and since it goes up, it must be sharp. Tell the children that a sharp is a half tone higher and a flat a half tone lower.

The question of tonality is very important. The pupil, in order really to think in the key, must feel the rest tone,* root tone, tonic or keynote, *i. e.*, the tone which rep-
Root Tone resents home, the tone which is the goal of all the other tones, and which the pupil must be conscious of in his playing and singing, so that he could stop at any time and give the keynote or tonic at once.

This point must be dwelt upon and made very clear; the pupil must perceive it, understand it and illustrate it.

In order to transpose in writing, the signatures must be explained. Teach one new signature at a time, using the following charts for mental imaging, and apply the knowledge at once by having the pupil transpose into the key whose signature has been learned.

* Also see ADDENDA, p. 53.

22

As soon as the scale is understood, let the pupil take a short melody and "find it" in the key of G, of F, of D—that is, sing, write and play it. A progressive drill in this transposing of melody should be a part of the daily work from now on, but always with the recognition of the keynote or root tone. Folk-music, especially the simplest French and German folk-songs, is the best material to use—but in the case of very young pupils, the shortest melodic phrases, such as the following, should be used:

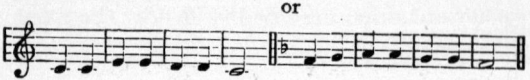

and here words, thought of either by the teacher or the pupil, are extremely useful, such as:

>Spring is here!
>Bloom like a rose!
>Rejoice and sing!

An illustration given by a child:

>"Little birdie, little birdie!
>   It is time to build your nest,
>For the winter now is over,
>   You must sing your very best."

As soon as possible, use Folk-music. Taking familiar tunes, such as "The Star-Spangled Banner," and transposing them at the keyboard is very helpful; but I find children woefully at a loss when asked for a song. It appears that American children, except those who attend the public schools, know practically no songs. "My Country, 'Tis of Thee" has been given me so often as the only song known, that my piano can almost play it of itself. We ought to sing more at home, as the Germans do.

Boys like the Wagner motifs, and the transposition of these motifs is helpful, both for the thought involved and the familiarity acquired with the best in music and literature. These motifs are really very simple, and neither teacher nor pupil need be terrified by the name of Wagner.

Use of Wagner Motifs

Siegfried's Motif.

The Rhine.

Walhalla.

This kind of work is necessarily slow, and in order to do it thoroughly more time should be allotted for the study of music; but, even as it is, a few moments taken from each lesson, and devoted to the thinking side of music, will be more than well spent.

During the first year or two, these seeds will produce no flowers that can be passed around to fond relatives and friends; but in the years to come, the garden will flourish, and there will be ample proof of the "worth-whileness" of it. My experience has been that the parents have become so interested in the children's work that they have taken up their own study of music once more, and found what they had been unable to grasp previously—an understanding of the fundamental principles—the principles of music which enabled them to use their knowledge and to enjoy it as they never had before.

This is one of the questions that I usually ask pupils of this kind: "Can **Thinking Scales** you think all scales and sing them, saying the name of the note, as the A scale (singing each tone) A, B, C♯, D, E, F♯, G♯, A?"

If not, drill in this way on every scale. Follow this with singing and playing of short original melodies in all keys, first singing and saying the scale. Think the melody, and sing exactly what you have thought, then write it and play it in all keys. When a grown person is asked whether she can do this, she usually says she can, but upon trying, she has trouble first of all in thinking a melody; secondly, in singing what she has thought; and thirdly, in remembering it long enough to write it down; finally she cannot play it.

Concentration and clear thinking are at the root of this drill, and I have seen women who have not studied at all since they left college or school really suffer over this work; but after a while they give thanks and are fascinated by the working of their own minds. Some thorough interval work is helpful at this point. Give the keynote on the piano and let the pupil sing any note you designate, as give C—ask the pupil to sing E (a third), G (a fifth), etc. Drill in all keys, keeping strictly to the intervals of the scale, in the following way:

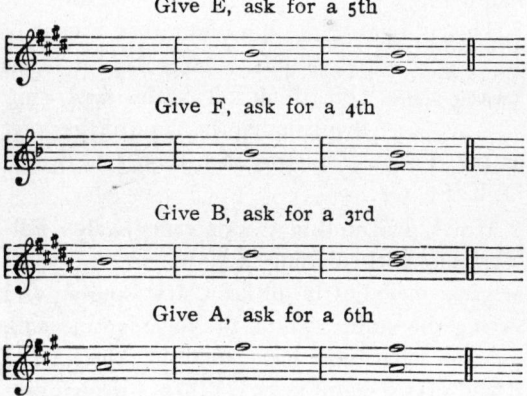

Let the pupil write out tables of intervals. Grown persons also are likely to be unconscious of the root-tone or keynote, and must be drilled on this. Dictation is a distinct help to transposition, *i. e.*, giving short phrases on the piano and having the pupil write them in different keys. Plan the work in this way— some dictation, some singing—a good deal of work at the keyboard.

Writing Tables of Intervals

Thus far we have dealt only with the melodic side of the question. In most cases it seems best to do this, but again there is no iron-clad rule, and if the harmonic side ("the bass") interests an older pupil more than the melodic does, work may be done there first as well as last.

To sum up what the pupil must have learned in order to transpose simple melodies into all keys; he must hear or think a melody; be conscious of the tonality or "home" tone, and of the scale relationship. He must be sure of the simple intervals as they occur in the scale and be able to sing the melody he has conceived, and to find it on the keyboard in all keys. If there is time, the sol fa syllables should be taught and used, but as time is usually so limited, it is better to use the ordinary alphabetical names.

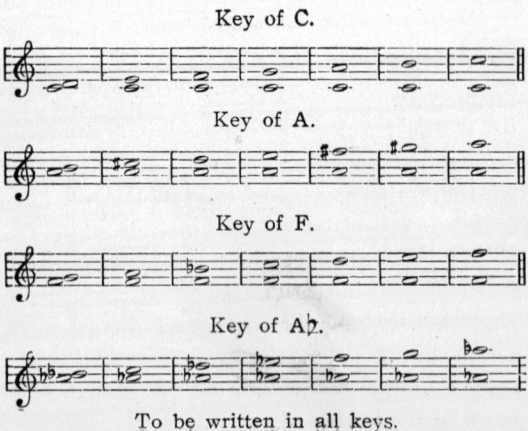

To be written in all keys.

CHAPTER III.

RHYTHM.

"The Hearing Ear and the Seeing Eye, the
Lord has made both of them."

HYTHM has been defined as the feeling that underlies music, the life or the motive power of tone. We cannot separate the sound from rhythm; for as soon as one thinks of or conceives a melody, it has rhythm. As soon as the musical idea takes form in the mind, motion becomes a part of it. There could be no melody without this thought of motion or rhythm—it is the very soul of musical expression and must be definitely conceived and understood. This, of course, is, first of all, a mental process.

Again we must listen and hear; and having heard consciously the melody and its rhythm, we must be able to express it definitely. Take for example this melody:

Where did it come from? I kept still and listened and finally heard it. That "something ever singing" that Browning speaks of, sang the song to me. I recognized melody and rhythm and I sang it. But how am I to express this rhythm of which I am inwardly conscious? Here is the melody, or rather, here are its tones:

In this form, however, it is a lifeless, motionless thing, yet I hear in my mind not the melody only, but the rhythm (motion). How am I to express this? By the help of what we call *time*.

When this has become a matter of definite knowledge, the next step is the expressing of rhythm (motion) that has been clearly thought out. In music there are in reality two rhythms only. One represents two and its multiples, the other three and its multiples. This is an important point; dwell on it! I use every expedient to develop this truth from the pupil, so that it is not simply a matter of information given by the teacher to the credulous pupil, but a matter of conviction, perception and understanding on the part of the intelligent pupil. It is worth while to take time to think out this question of rhythm. It is the very soul of music, and must be realized by the would-be musician. No person can realize rhythm for another—it must be realized in the mind of the student.

Rhythm the soul of Music

Let the child give (by clapping hands or tapping the foot) examples of two-pulse and three-pulse rhythm. Play waltzes and two-steps, and let him tell you which is which. Dwell on these simple rhythmic forms until they can readily be discerned by the pupil. Then take the next step. Let the pupil hear a melody and its rhythm, sing it—clapping hands or tapping the strong or accented tones or pulses. After this has become an easy matter—let him write the melody he has thought and sing it, and let him find and discover the time through the rhythm. "Time" is simply a mechanical aid, used to enable us to express rhythm. Tell him that the first note of every measure is apt to be the strong one, and that if he feels a strong tone, he must arrange his time so that the strong tone will fall on the first beat in the measure, as

This is of course elementary and not ideal. Musicians deplore the use of regular accentuation and insist upon more freedom but most teachers will agree with me in saying that to teach solely by phrases in the very beginning makes rhythm less clear to the pupils. (See ADDENDA.)

Dancing is invaluable as a help in arousing the sense of rhythm. Cecil J. Sharp, the famous

English authority on Folk Songs and Dances, has published several collections, which can be used. Playing these dances and asking the children to indicate the rhythm is another good way.

We must ask what makes the difference between 3/4 and 4/4 time, and *hope* that the pupil will be able to give the correct answer, i.e., that it all depends on the musical idea. If we are thinking our own original melodies, it depends upon the character of our idea, and if we are expressing the idea of Schumann or Beethoven, we must study to conceive and understand (and later to visualize) the composer's idea. In rhythm, as in melody, the sound or idea is the vital thing, and the time is the outcome of the sound.

The Musical Idea

In this study of rhythm words are often of great assistance. The strong accent, of course, comes on the important word, as

"The yeár's at the spríng,
The dáy's at the mórn."
R. B.

"The wórld is so fúll of a númber of thíngs
I'm súre we should áll be as háppy as kíngs!"
R. L. S.

But this is only a passing aid, since we are dealing with sound, and ultimately must feel the rhythm (motion) without the help of words.

There are other ways of helping children to realize rhythm, and dancing is one of the best. Needless to say this is popular with the children. (Also see ADDENDA.)

Several little pupils have told me that, thanks to this drill in rhythm, they have been promoted in dancing school. As soon as they get the consciousness of true rhythm in sound they are able to express it in the other arts.

When melody, rhythm and harmony become a conscious realization in the mind, musical education may honestly be said to have made a good beginning. Work done away from the piano at odd moments is invaluable, and older pupils have been able to think out this question of rhythm while they dressed or traveled to and fro on the cars. It is not what is done at the lesson that counts, but what is done in the mind of the pupil from day to day, or more correctly speaking, from minute to minute.

It will soon become evident that there are two kinds of tones in a musical idea: those that, through duration or accent, are more impressive, and those whose mission it is to adjust themselves to these more authoritative tones. The latter are commonly called "passing tones," and it is well to analyze in this way, finding the rest or accented tones, and then finding the passing tones, and expressing the music accordingly.

With children the idea of the family may be used again. The strong tone or home tone may be said to represent the mother in the scale; so in a melody, we may find the father, mother, aunt, etc., and all the children adjusting themselves obediently to the wishes of the elders.

DICTATION IN CONNECTION WITH RHYTHM

When the rhythm of your short original melodies can be felt, clapped, sung and played, you have made a good beginning. Dictation is a distinct help. With very small children, clapping, singing and playing make a good sequence, but children nine years old, or older, take dictation quite readily and enjoy it. Such a melody, for instance, as

Sleep, Baby, Sleep (Folk Song).

Dictate the melody to the pupil, letting him discover the rhythm for himself, tap or clap it, and write it as he feels it. This work is invaluable, and two or three students can help each other in this way—outside of the class. Let one student play the melody (on the piano), the others writing what they hear and feel, giving the rhythm; then let them express it in notes, putting in the time value, as

Theme from Allegretto from the VII Symphony of Beethoven.

Drill on rhythm should be kept up for a long time, and every help should be resorted to to make it clear.

Good melodies for dictation may be found in the Germer Edition of Folk Music, and in French Folk Songs. Folk songs are invaluable in teaching children to play, **Good Melodies for Dictation** and no child should ever be taught trashy music. "The best is good enough for me" might serve as a motto to teachers of children. Why should we wait until the musical taste is formed to bring out the love of the best and most beautiful in music? (See NOTE, p. 37.)

Older pupils may take up more difficult melodies as soon as they are able. Beethoven and Haydn Symphonies may be studied with great profit, taking up the different themes, and becoming mentally familiar with them.

PIANO WORK.

Of course the principle discovered all the way through must be applied to the student's regular piano work. The music he is playing must be the subject for thought, and a definite idea of the rhythm must be felt and expressed. Bach and Schumann have given plenty of material, after we have exhausted the available Folk-music. (SEE ADDENDA.)

Children should realize early the comparative meaninglessness of bars, and look for the musical idea, taking up simple music and analyzing the rhythm from this standpoint.

Schumann, Op. 68, No. 10.

Folk Song.

POWER OF CONTROLLED OR CONSTRUCTIVE THOUGHT.

We must learn to control our thinking, and utilize every waking moment in one of two things, constructive thought or constructive action. Turning the thing over in the mind is always of the greatest use, and in this work it is invaluable. Make a distinct mental effort in this direction every day, and watch the results.

Take one definite point, work it out patiently and thoroughly. Take rhythm until you understand that, and then take something else. This is the true "self-education," and the establishing of this balance between instruction and thought, constitutes (in my opinion) the only true education. Not the number of books you have read, but the thought you have given them, is what cultivates. Not the amount of instruction or the number of lessons you have taken will make of you an intelligent musician, but the thought, plus the work that you have given the problems your teacher has put before you, and the principle you have been enabled to discover.

NOTE. The teacher's special attention is called to the list of carefully selected pieces which may be used as teaching material, at the end of this book.

CHAPTER IV.

CHORDS.

INWARD hearing is again the root of this problem. The unity of melody, harmony and rhythm evidently exists in the mind, because as soon as a melody is heard and sung, almost invariably its harmony is heard also. The question is how to enable the pupil to perceive and understand this clearly. With children, teaching the simple tonic triad with each scale helps to establish an understanding. Let them listen while the teacher plays this simple triad, and then sing the strongest tone or root of such a chord as C, E, G. Play C, E, G separately, then together, and ask the child to sing you the home tone or root of it, which, of course, is C. After this is well established, let him find the other positions of the chord and play them, always singing the one root tone in this way:

Root Tones of Chords.

Sing C with each chord.

This drill must be kept up for a long time, until all tonic chords in their three positions are absolutely familiar. Then take a very simple melody, either the scale or such a melody as

Folk Song.

and ask the child to listen to what he hears with the do or G. Without doubt he will give you the G chord, thus:

and in the same way he will find the harmonies to the other melody notes, so that finally you will have

It is a fact then, that as soon as a tone is thought of or mentally heard its fundamental harmony is present in the mind and can be heard clearly also, if the pupil can learn to listen. I have tried this process on more than forty different persons, including a number of children. They did not all find it equally easy to listen, but after that became possible they all heard the same harmony, i.e., the simple fundamental harmony I, IV, V, I.

The simplest way of doing this is to play one tone of the scale and listen for its harmony. For instance, play C, listen and you will hear G and E. Play D, **A Tone and its Fundamental Harmony** listen, and you will hear B and G, etc. This chart illustrates the process imperfectly, because the listening may take longer than the note value given.

First hearing of the harmonization of the scale:

From this a clearer concept may be had by playing the fundamental (or root tone) with the chord, thus:

This is, however, very crude. The best way is the third, but since so many people find it simpler to use the second way, it is apparently a necessary step, and later the scale may be harmonized much more elaborately.

Those who have not tried and proved this will not believe it, but I know from experience that it is true. Children very rarely have any trouble in hearing harmonies. **Harmonization of Melodies** Older persons, who have given up in despair and are afraid to trust their "hearing ear," sometimes have to work longer with melody, but it always comes in the end, and since this is the basis of the harmonization of melodies it is worth striving for.

It is well to dictate simple melodies to children and to have them hear, sing and write the root tone to each melodic note. Here is a bass given me by a child eight years old after one winter's work:

In this case two children did the harmony together, one singing the melody and one the bass, and vice versa. Pupils should be drilled steadily in this until it becomes easy, and they can do it readily and quickly.

The next step is keyboard work. Give the child a short melody or melodic phrase at the keyboard, and let him find the bass. Drill on very elementary tunes until it

Harmonizing at Keyboard

becomes easy, and then let him take something he knows and likes and "find the bass." Folk music again and hymns, national airs and college songs are comparatively simple to harmonize. In three years pupils are usually able to take any tune they like and harmonize it in any key. But, of course, the time varies with the individual, and there is no rule. It is a matter of perception and drill.

Young children may be allowed to harmonize melodies simply by playing what they hear, but at eight or nine years the three fundamental harmonies underlying all music may be explained. First let the child play what he has heard and thought to be the bass he wants, then have him sing the root of each chord. For instance, take this melody,

French Folk Song.

Let him discover for himself that the first three notes of the melody call for the G chord as their bass, and that the root of the chord is therefore G. That the fourth note of the melody calls for the D chord as its bass, and that the root of the chord is therefore D (the dominant). That the fifth note calls again for the G chord, the root of which is G. The sixth for the D chord, etc. Let him put the name of the root of each chord under that chord. The first three being the same, will have g under them. The fourth being the D chord, finds its root on the fifth note of the scale, which is, of course, D. Ask for the notes of the chord. Thus the D chord is D, F-sharp, A. Accentuate the fact that this is the chord called the dominant, which chord is built on the fifth note of the scale.

Let him write out charts like the following, and be sure that he understands clearly that the three tonic chords are built with the notes of the triad, and that the three **Three Tonic** dominant chords are built from **Chords** the dominant triad, *i.e.*, the triad built with the dominant for its root-tone. This is most important.

G the dominant of C.

D the dominant of G.

F the dominant of B♭;

The fifth tone of the scale is called the Dominant and is next in importance to the home tone or keynote. Illustrate this by letting the pupil write basses to melodies that bring out this point, the teacher giving the melody, of course. For instance:

To bring out I – V – I.

Plenty of material may also be selected from German and French Folk Music.

Drill on this for some time, and also have the child play I, V, I in every key, first thinking the chord, thus:

Play I – V – I in every key.

    D   A   B♭

As soon as this has become absolutely clear, let him harmonize the three different positions of the two chords and write them out as follows, drilling in this way until the chords in all keys have been written and played.

Importance of Drill

Key of D.

  1st position.   2nd position.   3rd position.

Be sure that this is made perfectly clear. It is better to spend a long time and to drill too much than to neglect this point. I have found some very fair pianists painfully weak on this point, and these are the ones who cannot play a bass to "America."

After I, V, I becomes well established, explain IV, or the sub-dominant, in the same way, and drill for that as before, having the chords played in all keys, I, IV, I, and written out in this way. Be sure that the pupil can distinguish the dominant from the sub-dominant and think both correctly. Start the

The Sub-Dominant

drill as before, with the simple I, IV, I, to be written and played in all keys, thus:

and follow it with the harmonization of the three positions of the I, thus:

Key of C.
     1st position.   2nd position.   3rd position.

After this teach the child I, IV, V, I, and let him find this harmonic relationship in every key, and write it out. Then show the three positions as follows:

Key of D.

This is very crude, of course, and unmusical, but it is necessary in order to make the point clear.

From this point the pupil will be able to think and play simple basses to songs and tunes, and this being thoroughly worked out the older pupil can then, if he is inclined, enrich the harmonies to suit himself. It is best to keep the children to the fundamental harmonies.

Next take up the chord of the dominant seventh or V⁷. Explain it as the dominant chord with the seventh note added. If the pupil can instantly hear it (and many can), that is the best way to become acquainted with it. If not, play it and get the child to give its resolution or "home-coming." This is readily done. Then have him play chords of the dominant seventh in all keys and resolve them, writing them out thus:

Chord of the Dominant Seventh

To find Chord of the Dominant Seventh.
Key of C.

And if the previous work has been clearly understood this is not difficult. Let the pupil say what chord or harmony he is playing and write the figure under the bass as follows:

The Dominant Seventh and its resolution.
Key of G.   Key of D.   Key of F.   Key of C.

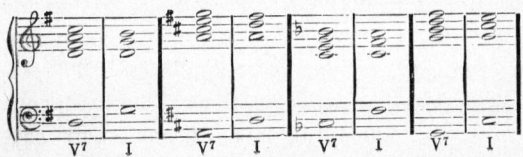

For children this is sufficient, but older students must be shown the other forms of the dominant seventh chords. Explain that just as the common chord of three tones may be presented in three different ways, thus

so the four-toned chord, called the dominant seventh, has four forms, i.e., one for each tone; and these different forms may be used according to the desire of the student, the root being, of course, always the same.

All dominant seventh chords, the root being C.

Have the older children and older pupils analyze Folk Music, giving the simple harmonies as they play them in this way:

Folk Song.

Folk music is the best, because in this there are no complex harmonies. This is, of course, very elementary work for older pupils, but for those who have not become con-

Value of Folk Music

scious of simple chord relationships these drills prove helpful, and, needless to say, make piano playing far more intelligent and thoughtful. It is not at all uncommon to have a pupil whom you have asked to tell you what some simple harmony she is playing is, answer quite naively, "I haven't the least idea." One older pupil came to me for help on a Beethoven Sonata. She played it well, technically, but with so little understanding that I was led to ask her whether she could play a simple melody and harmonize it. She clasped her hands rapturously and said:

"Oh, wouldn't it be wonderful to be able to do that!" She could not "pick out the treble" even of a child's song and give a respectable bass for it, and *she* is one of a thousand!

Major and Minor Modes.

In connection with the harmonizing of simple melodies, we must take up the subject of the major and minor modes. The root tone or tonic being the same, pupils should be taught to play minor triads by lowering the middle tone or third. They may be asked to tell the difference between a major and minor chord, and after they are able to think, sing, write and play both major and minor chords, knowing the difference and being able to tell which is major and which minor when you play it for them, let them practice writing and playing major and minor melodies and harmonizing them. After this teach them the minor scale.

Relative Minor and Natural Minor

This question of teaching the minor scale as a relative minor, relative to the scale three notes above it, is discussed a good deal by teachers. Musically, the so-called relative minor has "nothing to do with the case," but because it has borrowed its signature from its relative major it seems necessary to teach it. I usually let the pupil discover and find the natural minor scale, as, for instance, C major has C minor for its natural minor. Then I show them how in music the minor borrows its signature, and let them find music written in the minor mode and observe its signature, looking through some folk music or the Schumann Kinderscenen to find their minor signatures. Then I have them write out a table of the major and minor signatures, thus:

C major and A minor have the same signature.
G major and E minor have the same signature.
D major and B minor have the same signature.
A major and F sharp minor have the same signature.
E major and C sharp minor have the same signature.
B major and G sharp minor have the same signature.
F sharp major and D sharp minor have the same signature.
F major and D minor have the same signature.
B flat major and G minor have the same signature.
E flat major and C minor have the same signature.
A flat major and F minor have the same signature.
D flat major and B flat minor have the same signature.
G flat major and E flat minor have the same signature.

The way to play the so-called relative minor is to play the scale exactly as you would the major and raise the seventh tone a half-step. For instance, A is the relative minor to C.

Play a b c d e f g;
1 2 3 4 5 6 7

g being the seventh tone is raised a half step and is therefore *sharp*. G-sharp is, of course, followed by a —, and the scale is

This holds good for all the relative minor scales, of course.

Most children are quick at hearing major and minor intervals and chords, but in case they seem unable to distinguish between them keep up the drill until they can tell one from the other easily, especially the drill of playing a major or a minor chord and letting the pupil say what it is until he can finally hear inwardly and sing major and minor and is perfectly conscious of each mode.

The child learns thus how to think clearly; in other words, he learns how to study, as one child explained to me, "with his mind instead of with his eyes."

It is needless to say that this little book is not in any sense complete. It is simply suggestive of what may be done to make the

Studying with the Mind

thinking of music better understood. I have purposely refrained from discussing the alto and tenor voices, and the secondary chords, because the mental hearing of melody and the harmonizing of melodies in a simple way was the goal to be attained. If, after reaching this goal, the music lover is imbued with a desire to continue his study in this manner, he will be more than repaid and will, I trust, teach others to listen, sing and play so that in time there shall not be one soul that has not discovered the source of harmony and well-being which resides within himself.

ADDENDA

To page 17

Drills for visualizing:

1. **Five notes up.** 2. **Five notes down.**

3.   4.

5. **Scale up.**

6. **Scale down.**

7.

C chord.   Three positions of the C chord.

To page 21

Another good drill for hearing the rest tone or key-tone is for the teacher to play a phrase and, stopping just before the end, ask the pupil to sing the last note; for example:

Pupil to sing d

To page 31

Since writing this I have decided that it is pernicious to lay down this law. The best way to begin with the children is to have them indicate rhythms by lines, as

Baby bye, Here's a fly,

teaching the notation from the lines given by the child and thus showing the long and short notes.

To page 32

It is a good thing to ask the children to give you some example of rhythm in nature, or of anything rhythmic that they can think of. For rhythm the children have brought me the following answers:

Day and night.
The seasons.
The moon and the sun.
The waves.
The clock.
Breathing.

To page 36

Besides this, it is well to have a definite plan for teaching each piece; finding and singing each phrase, marking the fingering and pedaling, and making a simple harmonic sketch giving the I, IV, V, V^7 chords and changes of key.

TEACHING MATERIAL

Graded as to difficulty, Grade I being for beginners.

GRADE I

Schwalm, Easy Duets
Newton Swift, 12 Easy Pieces
Maxim, Noah's Ark
Czerny, Studies (Germer)
Forsman, Duets
Loomis, After the Lesson
Diabelli, Easy Duets
Gaynor, Miniatures
Cady, Folk-Melodies for Ten Fingers
Martin, Tone-Pictures
Gurlitt, Folk-Songs

GRADE II

Germer, Opus 34
Reinecke, Unsere Lieblinge
Gurlitt, Opus 117
Cady-Bach, Folk-Dances
Schumann, Opus 68
Czerny, Studies (Germer)
Tschaikowsky, Children's Album
Grieg, Opus 12
Reinhold, Miniatures
Heller, Op. 45, Op. 46, Op. 47
Hofer, Music in Child World, Vols. I-II
Kullak, Scenes from Childhood
Gaynor, Easy Pedal Studies
Burchenal-Crampton, Folk-Dances

GRADE III

Schumann, Opus 68
Heller, Op. 45, Op. 46, Op. 47

Hofer, Music in Child World, Vols. I-II
Kullak, Scenes from Childhood
Mozart, Minuet from Don Giovanni
Bach, Short Preludes and Fugues (Mason Ed.)
Händel, 12 Easy Compositions
Haydn, Easy Compositions
Beethoven, Easier Compositions
—— Minuet in E♭
—— Minuet in G major
Gluck, Album
Rebikow, Silhouettes
Ph. Em. Bach, Solfegietto
Schytte, Clown on Tight Rope
—— Hide and Seek
Händel, Largo without Octaves
Thorne, Forgotten Fairy Tales
—— Sonatina Album
Mendelssohn, Songs without Words

GRADE IV

Beethoven, Easier Compositions
—— Minuet in E
—— Minuet in G major
Debussy, Little Shepherd
—— Sonatina Album
Bach, Inventions
—— Sara Heintz Album
Grieg, Sailor's Song
—— Birdling
MacDowell, Woodland Sketches
Mendelssohn, Songs without Words
(Also Grade V)

MORE DIFFICULT

Bach, Suites
—— Well-Tempered Clavichord
—— Italian Concerto
—— Gavotte in B minor (Saint-Saëns Arr.)
—— Fantasie in C minor

Beethoven (Selected movements good to teach before an entire sonata is taken up)
    Opus 2, No. 2, Largo and Scherzo
    Opus 2, No. 3, Scherzo
    Opus 7, Largo
    Opus 10, No. 1, Adagio
    Opus 10, No. 2, Allegretto
    Opus 10, No. 3, Largo and Minuetto
    Opus 13, Adagio
    Opus 14, No. 2, Andante
    Opus 26, Theme
    Opus 27, No. 2, Adagio
    Opus 28, Andante
    Opus 31, No. 3, Allegretto and Minuetto
    Opus 49, No. 1
    Opus 49, No. 2
    Opus 57, Theme of Largo
    Opus 90, 2nd Movement
Brahms, Intermezzi, Op. 117 and Op. 118
—— B minor Capriccio
—— 2 Rhapsodies
—— Hungarian Dances
Chopin, Préludes
—— Waltzes
—— Études
—— Ballades
—— Impromptus
—— Mazurkas
—— Nocturnes and Fantaisies
—— Polonaises and Scherzo
Czerny, Opus 240, Opus 740
Daquin, Le Coucou
Gluck–Brahms, Gavotte
Gluck–Saint-Saëns, Air from Alceste (Joseffy Arr.)
Mendelssohn, 2 Préludes in E minor
—— Nocturne from "Midsummer Night's Dream"
—— Rondo capriccioso
—— Scherzo

Mozart, Sonatas in C major, G major
—— Fantasies
—— Pastorale varié in B♭
—— Minuet from E♭ Symphony
Schubert, Marche Militaire
—— Impromptus
—— Minuet in B minor
—— Moments Musicaux
—— Sonatas
Schumann, Opus 15
—— Novelletten
—— Fantasiestücke
—— Albumblätter
—— Romance in F♯ major
—— Nachtstücke
—— Papillons
—— Carnaval
Scarlatti, Album, 22 pieces
Sgambati, Gavotte in A♭ minor

(Supplementary List)

Rubinstein, Kamennoi Ostrow
—— Barcarolle
—— Romance in E♭
Rachmaninoff, Préludes
—— Polichinelle
Tschaikowsky, Song without Words in F major
—— Chanson triste
—— Barcarolle
—— Romance in F minor
Debussy, Children's Corner
—— 2 Arabesques
—— Reverie
—— Suite Bergamasque
—— Préludes
Grieg, Sonata
—— Lyrics (5 books)
Slav Album, Vols. I and II
Album of Russian Music, Vols. I and II

Scandinavian Album
MacDowell, Sea Pieces
—— Tarantella
—— Scotch Poem
—— Improvisations
—— Hexentanz
—— Shadow Dance
D'Albert, Gavotte and Musette
Sibelius, Romance in D♭
Scriabine, Nocturne for left hand
Paderewski, Cracovienne
—— Mélodie in G♭
—— Chant du Voyageur
Rameau, Album (Litolf Ed.)
Paradies, Toccata
Couperin, Album
Moszkowski, Album
Saint-Saëns, Romance in B minor
Strauss, Träumerei in B major
Stojowski, Waltz in E♭
—— Chant d'Amour